THE BREAKUP
OF
YUGOSLAVIA

Martyn Rady

New York

Conflicts

Titles in the series:
The Breakup of the Soviet Union
The Breakup of Yugoslavia
Conflict in Eastern Europe
Conflict in Somalia and Ethiopia
Conflict in Southern Africa
Conflict in the Middle East

Cover: Croatian soldiers defend their position in a ruined house, 1991.

Title page: Sarajevo, September 1992: hurrying to escape Serbian snipers and artillery fire.

Picture acknowledgments
The publishers would like to thank the following for supplying their photographs for use as illustrations in this book:
Camera Press Ltd. *cover* (Eastlight), 16, 22 (Klaus Lehnartz), 23, 30 (Eastlight), 37 (Sir Russell Johnson), 38 (Sir Russell Johnson); Eye Ubiquitous 4; Frank Spooner Pictures 41 (Gamma/Reid Andrew), 44 (Gamma/Art Zamur); Rex Features 1 (Sipa), 5 (Sipa), 6 (Sipa/Alpha Diffusion), 8 (Sipa/Alexandra Boulat), 9 (Tom Haley), 13, 14, 17 (Sipa/Srdan Petrovic), 18, 19, 20 (Sipa/Alexandra Boulat), 24 (Sipa/Alexandra Boulat), 25 (Eastlight/Arno Schaden), 26 (Zullo), 27, 28 (Futy-Sipa), 29 (Sipa/Luc Delahaye), 31 (Sipa/Andre Kaiser), 32 (Tim Rooke), 33 (Sipa/Alexandra Boulat), 34 (Luc Delahaye), 35, 36 (Sipa/Eastlight), 39 (Sipa/Andre Kaiser), 40 (Sipa/Joe Tabacca), 42 (Sipa/Argyropoulos), 45 (Maecke); Topham Picture Source 11, 12, 15, 21, 43 (Associated Press).
Maps on pages 7 and 10, and the artwork on page 8 were supplied by Peter Bull.

Editor: Judy Martin
Series editor: William Wharfe
Designer/Typesetter: Malcolm Walker/Kudos Editorial and Design Services

First American publication 1994 by New Discovery Books,
Macmillan Publishing Company, 866 Third Avenue, New York, NY 10022

Macmillan Publishing Company is part of the
Maxwell Communication Group of Companies.

First published in 1994 by Wayland (Publishers) Ltd
61 Western Road, Hove, East Sussex BN3 1JD

Library of Congress Cataloging-in-Publication Data

Rady, Martyn C.
    The breakup of Yugoslavia / Martyn Rady.
        p. cm.—(Conflicts)
    Includes bibliographical references and index.
    ISBN   0-02-792529-3
    1. Yugoslavia—History—Juvenile literature. 2. Yugoslav War,
1991—Juvenile literature. [1. Yugoslavia—History. 2. Yugoslav
War, 1991–] I. Title. II. Series
DR1246.6.R33 1994
949.7—dc20   93-40592
    Summary: Provides an in-depth look at the current turmoil in
the former country of Yugoslavia.

Printed and bound in Italy by G. Canale & C.S.p.A., Turin

Contents

CHAPTER 1

INTRODUCTION

In the 1970s and 1980s, Yugoslavia seemed quite unlike the drab communist countries elsewhere in Eastern Europe. Visitors to its cities noticed the well-dressed people, the busy stores, and the streets bustling with traffic. Tourists who spent their holidays in luxury hotels at one of the resorts along the Adriatic coast were usually full of praise.

Western politicians and diplomats shared this high opinion of Yugoslavia. Yugoslavia's leaders gave every appearance of being sensible and moderate men. Unlike the rulers of other communist states, they were friendly toward Western countries. Yugoslavia seemed a stable country, well worth supporting.

These appearances were, however, misleading. In reality, Yugoslavia was a police state, where

With its medieval churches and narrow streets, the ancient port of Dubrovnik on Yugoslavia's Adriatic coast was a popular resort for vacationers in the 1970s and 1980s.

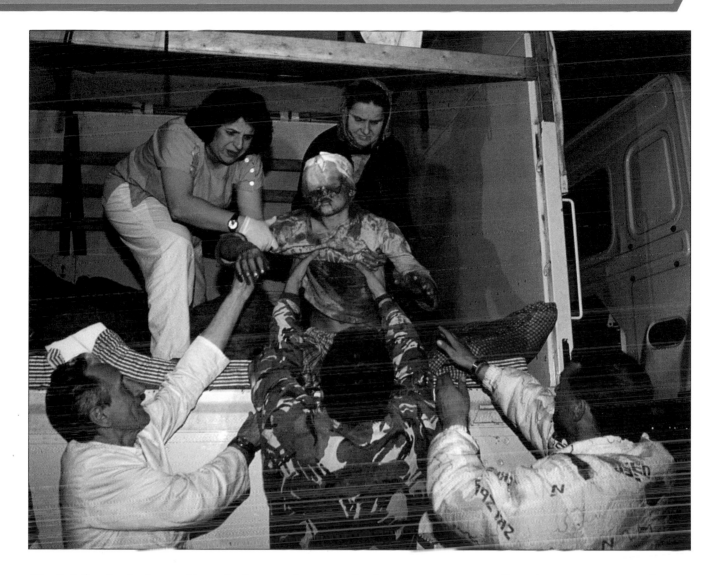

The fighting in the former Yugoslavia created a wave of refugees. By 1993 more than three million people had been made homeless. Not all the refugees were able to find safety. For many, like these Bosnian Muslims, the only shelter available was in crowded cities where they remained under attack from Serbian gunmen.

people could be imprisoned for their beliefs. Only one political party was allowed: the Communist party. All the rest were banned. The country's prosperity was largely due to the vast amount of money the government had managed to borrow from abroad. Furthermore, this borrowed wealth was unevenly spread. Although people in many of the cities lived well enough, many people in large parts of the countryside suffered from poverty. In rural areas, especially in the south, Yugoslavia had much more in common with its neighbors in the Balkans—Albania, Bulgaria, and Romania—than with Western Europe.

Most importantly, the peoples of Yugoslavia were divided. Serbs, Croats, Slovenes, Muslims, Montenegrins, Albanians, and Macedonians— all of whom made up the population of Yugo- slavia—were suspicious and resentful of one another. Bad feelings among these separate peoples began to grow in the late 1980s and suddenly exploded into violence in 1991. Almost overnight, the world's perception of Yugoslavia changed. From being a peaceful, serene, and stable country, Yugoslavia suddenly became a land of murder and refugees.

The chapters that follow will tell you why and how this happened.

PEOPLES, LANGUAGES, AND RELIGIONS

A federal state
After World War II, in 1945, Yugoslavia was organized as a federal republic, similar to the United States. Although the central government in Belgrade still held supreme authority, an element of home rule was allowed to the six republics that made up Yugoslavia: Serbia, Croatia, Slovenia, Bosnia-Herzegovina, Macedonia, and Montenegro. The powers of the governments of the six republics were greatly extended in 1974.

Yugoslavia means "the land of the South Slavs." Most of the population of the former Yugoslavia are South Slavs: Serbs, Croats, Slovenes, Macedonians, and Montenegrins. All of these population groups, or "nationalities," speak languages that are closely related to one another, and which can generally be understood by other South Slav speakers. The Serbian and Croatian languages are, in fact, so close that they are often referred to as a single language, called Serbo-Croat.

Among the South Slavs, language is often considered the main mark of nationality, but religious beliefs are probably just as important. Since the Middle Ages, when they were converted to Christianity, the Serbs, Montenegrins, and Macedonians have belonged to the Eastern Orthodox religion. They therefore share the same faith as the Russian, Greek, Romanian, and Bulgarian Christians. As a consequence, they write with Cyrillic letters, as these form the alphabet used in the religious

A man in Belgrade, the capital of Serbia, reads a newspaper printed in Cyrillic. The Cyrillic alphabet is used throughout Serbia, Montenegro, and Macedonia.

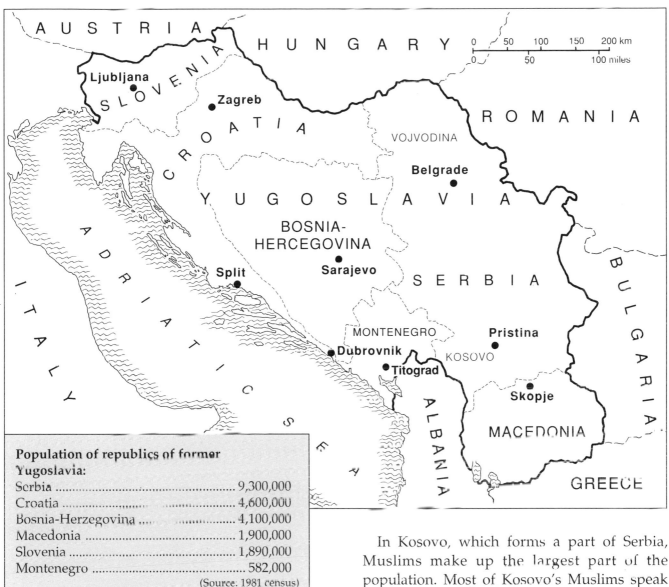

Population of republics of former Yugoslavia:	
Serbia	9,300,000
Croatia	4,600,000
Bosnia-Herzegovina	4,100,000
Macedonia	1,900,000
Slovenia	1,890,000
Montenegro	582,000
(Source: 1981 census)	

services of the Orthodox church. By contrast, the Slovenes and Croats were converted in the Middle Ages to Roman Catholicism. As a result, they use Roman letters—the alphabet in which this book is written.

For 500 years, from the fourteenth to the nineteenth centuries, a large part of Yugoslavia was included in the Ottoman Turkish empire. As a result of the long period of Turkish occupation, about an eighth of the population of the former Yugoslavia is Muslim. Although spread throughout Yugoslavia, the Muslim population is heavily concentrated in two areas: Kosovo and Bosnia-Herzegovina.

In Kosovo, which forms a part of Serbia, Muslims make up the largest part of the population. Most of Kosovo's Muslims speak Albanian, which is not related to any other language used in Yugoslavia. In Bosnia-Herzegovina, Muslims make up 40 percent of the population. Although the Muslims of Bosnia-Herzegovina are frequently referred to as Bosnians, there is no Bosnian language as such. The Muslims of Bosnia-Herzegovina speak mainly Serbian or Croatian, although some use Albanian.

At the end of World War II, the state of Yugoslavia was organized as a federation of six republics: Slovenia, Croatia, Serbia, Bosnia-Herzegovina, Montenegro, and Macedonia. Although Serbia and Montenegro currently remain united in a joint state that still calls itself Yugoslavia, in 1991 and 1992 the other

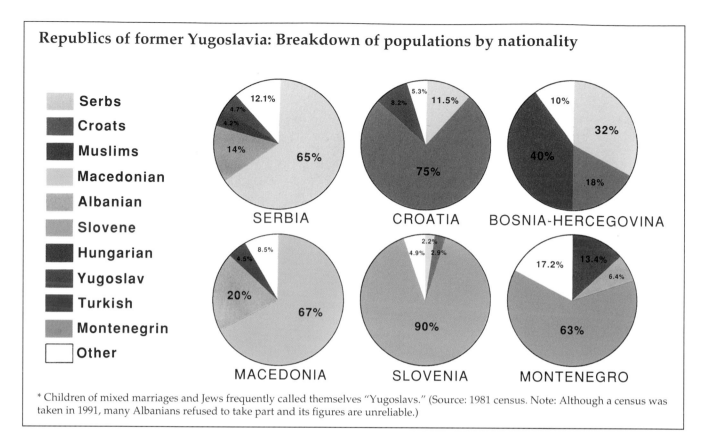

Republics of former Yugoslavia: Breakdown of populations by nationality

Legend:
- Serbs
- Croats
- Muslims
- Macedonian
- Albanian
- Slovene
- Hungarian
- Yugoslav
- Turkish
- Montenegrin
- Other

SERBIA: 65%, 14%, 4.2%, 4.7%, 12.1%

CROATIA: 75%, 8.2%, 5.3%, 11.5%

BOSNIA-HERCEGOVINA: 40%, 10%, 32%, 18%

MACEDONIA: 67%, 20%, 4.5%, 8.5%

SLOVENIA: 90%, 4.9%, 2.2%, 2.9%

MONTENEGRO: 63%, 17.2%, 13.4%, 6.4%

* Children of mixed marriages and Jews frequently called themselves "Yugoslavs." (Source: 1981 census. Note: Although a census was taken in 1991, many Albanians refused to take part and its figures are unreliable.)

republics declared themselves to be fully independent states.

The populations of the republics of Slovenia and Croatia are largely Slovene and Croat. Serbia, Montenegro, and Macedonia are more mixed. In these republics, Serbs, Montenegrins, and Macedonians make up only two-thirds of the population, the remainder consisting largely of Albanian speakers and, in Serbia, of Hungarian speakers as well. Bosnia-Herzegovina has, however, always been a complete hodgepodge where no single nationality forms a majority. The various elements of the population—Muslims, Serbs, and Croats—are intermingled and pocketed throughout the republic.

In the former Yugoslavia, however, the cultural division between town and country has often influenced attitudes as powerfully as divisions of language and of religion. For most of their history, the peoples of Yugoslavia lived on the land. The towns were small and homes only of foreign merchants, government officials, and tax collectors. Although this situation began to change with the onset of industrial growth early

Agriculture in Yugoslavia was carried out on small plots worked by peasant farmers. They often lacked modern equipment, such as tractors, and instead had to use horses for plowing.

A Croatian proverb
"You can eat with a Serb, drink with a Serb, but you cannot turn your back on a Serb."

in the twentieth century, older attitudes have remained. Country people in the former Yugoslavia still tend to regard town dwellers as money-grubbing, selfish, and irreligious. For their part, townsfolk commonly consider the rural population to be lazy and superstitious.

Conflict among the nationalities of former Yugoslavia was made worse by this traditional distrust felt by country folk for the townspeople. Serbia (particularly in the south), Montenegro, and Macedonia are still heavily rural, and much of their population consists of peasant farmers. Croatia and Slovenia are more urban and industrialized. In Bosnia-Herzegovina, while the Muslims tend to congregate in the towns, Serbs dominate in the countryside. The fury with which armed Serbian peasants bombarded Sarajevo, the capital of Bosnia-Herzegovina, in 1992 and 1993, and the pleasure Montenegrin highlanders took in devastating the luxury hotels and duty-free shops along the Dubrovnik coast in 1991, had their origin in the peasantry's contempt for city life.

The name *Yugoslavia* thus concealed a bewildering mixture of languages, religions, cultures, and even alphabets. Unlike Italy, Germany, or France, "the land of the South Slavs" was not a nation-state, but a state of many nationalities. Religion, culture, and alphabet served to deepen divisions among the national groups. Language was thus only one part of a very complex equation separating one group of people from another.

Although for long periods the various nationalities of Yugoslavia lived in apparent peace, tensions were always present. At times of stress, ill feelings always had a way of bubbling to the surface. In the early 1990s, as the country moved into deep political crisis, the complex divisions that still separated the peoples of Yugoslavia tore apart the state in which they lived.

Artillery shells hit buildings in Sarajevo.

Hatreds in Sarajevo
"Followers of three different faiths—Muslim, Roman Catholic, and Orthodox—they hated one another from the day of their birth to their death. . . . They were born, they grew up and died in this hate, this actual revulsion towards a neighbour of another faith. Whenever, due to some great or calamitous event, the established order was shaken, all the long-suppressed hatreds and secret hankerings for destruction and violence broke to the surface."
(*The Woman from Sarajevo*, Ivo Andrić, 1966)

THE MAKING OF YUGOSLAVIA

Until this century, the territory of Yugoslavia comprised a number of separate kingdoms and principalities, most of which were under foreign domination.

Ever since the Middle Ages, Croatia had belonged to the kingdom of Hungary. Hungary itself was part of the Austrian, or Hapsburg, empire. From the late eighteenth century, Montenegro was an independent mountain state ruled over by its own prince. Slovenia, however, did not exist at all; the land in which the Slovenes lived was made up of the Austrian provinces of Carniola and Carinthia. Serbia, Bosnia-Herzegovina, and Macedonia were all parts of the Ottoman Turkish empire.

During the nineteenth century, as the power of the Ottoman Turkish empire declined, an independent Serbian kingdom had been established. The rulers of Serbia were ambitious. They planned to replace the Ottoman empire in the Balkans with a greatly enlarged Serbian

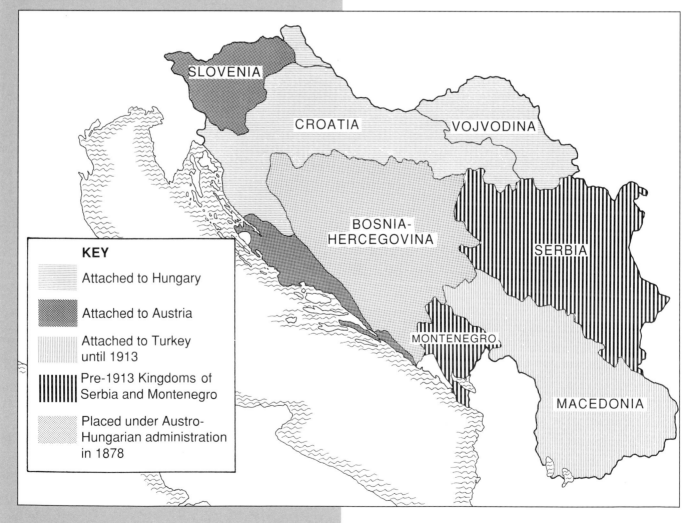

KEY

	Attached to Hungary
	Attached to Austria
	Attached to Turkey until 1913
	Pre-1913 Kingdoms of Serbia and Montenegro
	Placed under Austro-Hungarian administration in 1878

The Yugoslav kingdom was formed from states that previously had quite separate identities.

The Austrian archduke Franz Ferdinand and the archduchess Sophie visiting the town hall of Sarajevo on June 28, 1914. Within less than an hour, both were assassinated by a Bosnian Serb student.

kingdom. They coveted, in particular, the Turkish-run territories of Bosnia-Herzegovina and Macedonia. In 1878, however, Bosnia-Herzegovina was taken over by the Austrians. Serbian interest thus rapidly became concentrated on Macedonia.

In 1903, the Macedonians launched a massive revolt against Turkish rule. The Turks, however, suppressed the uprising with such ferocity that the Austrians and Russians felt obliged to intervene to protect the province's Christian population. Two years later, the Turkish ruler, or sultan, was made to agree both to the division of Macedonia into districts based on nationality and to the presence in Macedonia of an international peacekeeping force.

The international force, which included British, French, and Italian soldiers, failed to stop the violence. Furthermore, as Turks and

Macedonians fought to establish complete control of the districts that they had been given, the conflict became more bloody. As a result of its failure, the international force had to be withdrawn, and Macedonia was briefly returned to weak Turkish rule. (Sadly, the lesson of Macedonia was overlooked by those Western diplomats who in the 1990s tried to impose an almost identical scheme on war-torn Bosnia-Herzegovina.) The solution to the Macedonian problem, eventually reached during the Balkan Wars in 1912–1913, was that Macedonia was partitioned among Serbia, Greece, and Bulgaria, with Serbia taking the lion's share.

The rulers of the neighboring Austrian Hapsburg empire became concerned by Serbia's success. When, in 1914, the heir to the Austrian throne, the archduke Franz Ferdinand, was assassinated in Sarajevo by a Bosnian Serb, the

> **Report of atrocities in Macedonia**
> "During April 1905 an old man, Gheorghe Jantcheff, was killed in the village of Messimer by the [Turkish] soldiers stationed there. To explain their whim, the soldiers declared that they had met him carrying food to the [Macedonian] insurgents. Now not a crumb of bread was found on the corpse nor in its proximity. The soldiers were not proceeded against for their crime."
>
> (*Macedonia and the Reforms*, Draganof, 1908)

Austrians seized the chance to punish Serbia. By declaring war on Serbia, a country supported by Austria's enemy, Russia, the Hapsburg empire unleashed World War I (1914–1918).

During the late eighteenth and nineteenth centuries, a sense of common South Slav nationhood had been promoted by politicians and thinkers in the Balkans. It had been argued that since the Slovenes, Serbs, Croats, Macedonians, and Montenegrins spoke similar languages, they formed in reality a single nation and should therefore be given their own united state.

The slogan of *Jugoslavija*—of one Yugoslav state for all the South Slavs—became increasingly popular as the war dragged on, appealing even to the Muslims of Bosnia-Herzegovina. Although some Serbian politicians saw in the idea of Yugoslavia a way of extending Serbia's territory, for a short period there was genuine and widespread enthusiasm for the creation of a single state bringing together all the South Slavs.

Using the murder of the archduke Franz Ferdinand as an excuse, the Austrian government declared war on Serbia on July 28, 1914. In this photograph, taken in Belgrade shortly before the declaration of war, Serbs read the order instructing soldiers to report to barracks. Within a week, nearly all of Europe was at war.

In 1903, Peter I Karadjordjević took power in Serbia following a military coup, during which the previous king and queen were brutally murdered. In 1918, Peter became the first monarch of a united South Slav state.

In 1918, the Austrian Hapsburg and German empires were defeated. With the support of the victorious allies, a new Yugoslav state was founded. The new state united Serbia, Macedonia, Croatia, Carniola and southern Carinthia (those parts of Austria where the Slovene population lived), and southern Hungary (where the majority of the population was Serbian). Montenegro, having deposed its ruler, also chose to join the new state.

The new state, proclaimed in 1918, was not at first called Yugoslavia. Instead, it went by the name of the Kingdom of Serbs, Croats, and Slovenes. Although omitting the Macedonians and Montenegrins, the name was intended to make the point that the new state existed for the equal benefit of all the South Slavs.

It rapidly became clear, however, that the Kingdom of Serbs, Croats, and Slovenes existed primarily for the benefit of the Serbs. The monarch of the new kingdom, Peter I Karadjordjević, had, since 1903, been king of Serbia; the capital was Belgrade, which was also the capital of Serbia; the parliament was dominated by Serbians; and the powerful army and civil service were largely staffed by Serbian officers and officials. Neither the Croats nor the Slovenes were permitted any form of home rule, to which the Croats in particular thought themselves entitled; all important political decisions were made instead by Serbs in Belgrade.

Croatian politicians, in particular, resented the influence of the Serbs in the new state. As they voiced their criticisms ever more noisily in the parliament in Belgrade, its sessions rapidly dissolved into exchanges of insults and fisticuffs. In 1928, two leading Croatian politicians were shot dead by a Montenegrin member of

CHAPTER 3

Medieval Serbia
In the Middle Ages, there was an independent Serbian kingdom that, in the fourteenth century, controlled most of the Balkans. Although this empire was destroyed by the Turks in 1389, Serbs have always remembered that once they were members of a mighty kingdom. The Croats also experienced a brief period of medieval greatness—back in the tenth and eleventh centuries. None of the other peoples of Yugoslavia has any such independent state to look back on, although the mountain kingdom of Montenegro was never completely conquered by the Turks.

parliament in the middle of a debate. The next year, the king closed down the parliament and took over the running of the country as a dictator.

Peter's successor, King Alexander (1921–1934), genuinely wanted to rule a united kingdom. To try to make his subjects forget their old identities and instead think of themselves as a single people, Alexander changed the name of the state to Yugoslavia in 1929. He established his own political organization, the Yugoslav National party, in which he tried to involve both Serbian and non-Serbian politicians. Entirely new administrative districts, named after rivers, were formed in the hope that people might, in time,

Prince Alexander of Serbia, who became monarch of the Kingdom of the Serbs, Croats, and Slovenes in 1921, is shown here visiting Paris during World War I. Alexander's attempt to create a nation of "Yugoslavs" was destined to fail. He was assassinated in 1934.

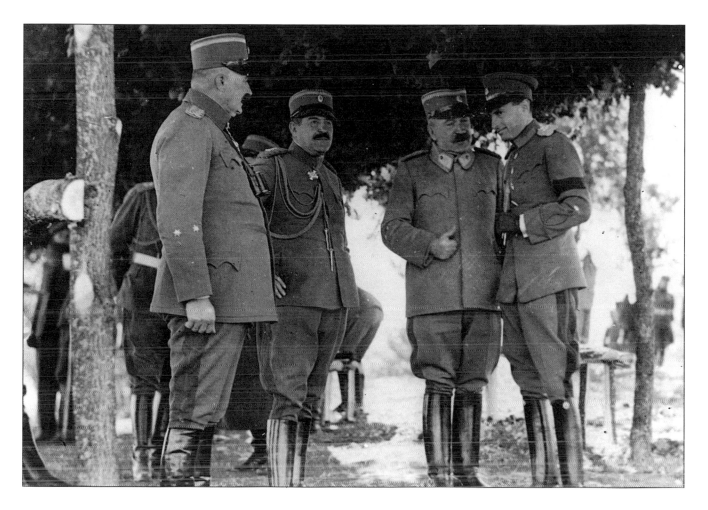

Wearing a mourning band in memory of the murdered King Alexander, the regent, Prince Paul (far right), attends military maneuvers in 1935. As it turned out, the Yugoslav army and its generals proved no match for the Germans in 1941.

forget their older national homelands.

Alexander failed to realize that nations cannot be created or suppressed by orders from above. Despite the change of name to Yugoslavia, the king found it impossible to create Yugoslavs. Instead, the peoples of Yugoslavia continued to think of themselves as being first and foremost Serbs, Croats, or Slovenes. Instead of healing divisions, Alexander's government only made them worse, for now it seemed that the king wanted to destroy the special sense of belonging to a historic people.

In 1934, Alexander was assassinated, while on a state visit to France, by orders of extremist Croatian leaders. His successor, Peter II, was only eleven years old at the time of his father's assassination. For this reason Alexander's cousin,

Prince Paul, was appointed regent and took power.

Paul ruled in a far less dictatorial way than Alexander. He tried to reach an agreement with the Croatian politicians, who were the firmest in their opposition to rule from Belgrade.

In August 1939, Croatia was put back on the map and granted home rule. This, however, only angered the Serbian politicians, who saw no reason why Croatia should be given such a privileged position in Yugoslavia. The outbreak of World War II in September 1939 prevented further attempts to solve the national rivalries in Yugoslavia. Instead, the war brought to the surface the seething hatreds that King Alexander and Prince Paul had sought to smother.

WAR AND THE COMMUNIST TAKEOVER

In April 1941, Germany invaded Yugoslavia. Peter II, who had just been declared old enough to rule without a regent, fled abroad. Yugoslavia was then broken up by Hitler, and large chunks of its territory were given to Germany's allies. Montenegro was given to Italy, and Macedonia was divided between Bulgaria and Italian-ruled Albania. Hungary received parts of northern Serbia. Slovenia was partitioned between Germany and Italy.

In Serbia and Croatia, Hitler set up puppet governments. Of these, the Croatian *Ustaša*, or fascist government, was the more fanatical. Once in power, the *Ustaša* began an immediate policy of removing the Serbian Orthodox population from Croatian soil. With the slogan "One-third exterminated, one-third deported, one-third converted," the *Ustaša* organized massacres and placed many tens of thousands of Serbs in concentration camps. The exact number of Serbs murdered by the *Ustaša* is reckoned to have been about a third of a million, but Serbs tend to believe the death toll was much higher.

The occupations by the Germans and Italians, and the Croatian *Ustaša*, were both resisted by

These soldiers from a Croatian Ustaša *unit celebrate a massacre of Serbian civilians. The Croats were often joined by Muslim fighters. On occasions, however, Croats put on the typical Muslim headdress, the fez, so as to cause hatred between Muslims and Serbs.*

Recalling the bitter civil war of 1941–1945, over forty years later a Serbian Orthodox priest solemnly reburies the bones of 600 Serbs killed by Croatian Ustasa troops in 1941.

guerrilla fighters. The guerrillas were gathered in two main groups: the Chetniks (whose name comes from the Serbian word for regiment) and the partisans. The Chetniks consisted almost entirely of Serbs and were dedicated to the restoration of Serbian and royal government. The partisans drew their support from both the Serbian and non-Serbian populations and were organized by the Communist leader, Josip Broz Tito.

Tito (1892–1980), the son of a Croat father and Slovene mother, was a lifelong Communist who had fought with the Red Army in Russia. A locksmith and mechanic by training, he was also an excellent organizer. As secretary of the Yugoslav Communist party from 1937, he had built the party up from a few hundred members to over 10,000 by 1941. In the space of the fifteen

months following the German invasion of Yugoslavia, Tito organized a resistance army of 150,000 volunteers.

The strategies of the partisans and the chetniks differed. The Chetniks held back from fighting the Germans. They preferred to wait for the time when the Allies would begin the liberation of the country. The savagery of German reprisals—100 civilians shot for every German soldier killed—further discouraged the Chetniks from taking decisive military action.

By contrast, Tito coldly calculated that German reprisals would benefit his guerrilla force, for the atrocities would be bound to turn the population against the invaders and so swell the number of his partisans. Nevertheless, throughout the war, the principal targets of Tito's partisans were as much the Chetniks, the *Ustaša*, and the forces loyal to the puppet government in Belgrade, as the Germans and Italians. In 1943, Tito even tried to reach a deal with Hitler, whereby the Germans would give the partisans a free hand to pursue their war with the Chetniks. Tito was already preparing for the day when the war would be over. Aiming to seize power as head of a communist government, Tito was anxious to eliminate all possible opposition.

The fighting in Yugoslavia during World War II was therefore not simply a war against the Germans and Italians, but also a civil war in which partisans killed Chetniks and the *Ustaša* murdered Serbs. By 1945, four years of conflict had claimed the lives of 1.2 million people in Yugoslavia, or 10 percent of the country's population. Of this 1.2 million, it is estimated that the majority were killed by fellow Yugoslavs.

In October 1944, the Soviet army entered Yugoslavia from the northeast, and Belgrade was liberated by a joint Soviet and partisan force.

Despite their wild and tough-looking appearance, the Chetniks failed to take on the German and Italian forces occupying Yugoslavia. Most of their operations were aimed instead against Tito's partisans and the Croatian Ustaša.

> **Orders from Tito, March 30, 1943**
> "Actions against the Germans would not serve the interests of our present operations. Our most important task is to destroy the Chetniks and their administrative apparatus which represents the greatest danger for the further development of the people's liberation struggle."

The army then left Yugoslavia, wheeling north toward Germany. The partisans were thus left with the responsibility of freeing the remainder of the country from the Germans, a task completed in May 1945.

With the end of the war, Yugoslavia largely returned to its old frontiers. However, the country's politics changed entirely from what it was before, between the two world wars.

In March 1945, the Allies compelled King Peter to appoint Tito as premier. As the leader of the largest and most powerful military force in Yugoslavia, it was thought impossible to give Tito any lesser office. Tito immediately installed a government dominated by Communists. In November 1945, he held a rigged election that returned a Communist majority to the parliament. The parliament immediately abolished the monarchy and adopted a constitution based on that of the Soviet Union.

Over the next few years, the Yugoslav Communists tried to turn their country into an exact copy of the Soviet Union, which was regarded at the time as the model for a communist country. The only political party allowed to function in Yugoslavia was the Communist party. Opposition politicians were arrested or forced to flee abroad. Those classed as traitors or war criminals were executed after show trials. The churches were ruthlessly suppressed.

In imitation of the Soviet Union, Tito also started a five-year plan. The purpose of the plan was to make Yugoslavia a modern, industrial country. The building of factories was started in Macedonia, Montenegro, and Bosnia-Herzegovina, all of which had previously depended on agriculture. At the same time, the

After the German invasion of Yugoslavia, the British government, led by Winston Churchill (center), backed the chetniks. In 1943, Churchill and the Allies switched their support to Tito (left). Churchill forced King Peter's government-in-exile, led by Ivan Subašić (right), to agree to Tito becoming prime minister.

government started to organize the peasantry into large state farms or collectives. The five-year plan was so ambitious and detailed that, when printed, it weighed over 3,000 lbs. (1,360 kgs.).

The Soviet leader, Joseph Stalin, resented Tito's attempt to make Yugoslavia a modern industrial country. He wanted to keep the Yugoslav economy mainly agricultural, to provide cheap food for the Soviet Union. He aimed, too, to put the Yugoslav army under Soviet control, and to install his agents in commanding positions in the Yugoslav party, government, and secret police. Tito refused, however, to knuckle under to Stalin and so, in 1948, Yugoslavia was expelled from the Soviet bloc. Tito then began to pursue an independent foreign policy of friendliness toward the West.

The split between Tito and Stalin took place at the time when the cold war was at its height. As a consequence, Tito was rewarded by the United States with relief supplies, armaments, and, eventually, massive loans. These contributed to the success of Tito's plans to modernize the Yugoslav economy.

> **Civil war in Yugoslavia**
> "All of them: *Ustaša*, Chetniks, Serbs, Croats and Muslims killed each other and when the knife is used, there is no difference between a cross, crescent, a letter U or a red star: the pain is the same. The partisans too divided us into rich and poor peasants, into middle class and worker, into progressive and reactionary, and killed accordingly."
>
> (*The Knife*, V. Drašković, 1982)

TITO'S YUGOSLAVIA

Following the break with the Soviet Union in 1948, Tito moderated his policy of rapid industrial growth. The planning system was largely abandoned. Instead, a program of "self-management" by councils of workers was introduced into factories. The idea behind "self-management" was that the workers themselves would decide on production targets and wage levels. Although in reality the Communist party still kept considerable control of the economy, self-management seemed to work. During the 1950s and 1960s, the Yugoslav economy grew at a faster rate than ever before, and the peoples of Yugoslavia entered into a period of increasing prosperity.

In several crucial respects, however, the economic success story of Tito's Yugoslavia was a lie. In order to keep the population content, the country imported far more foreign consumer goods than it could possibly afford. The trade imbalance was made up for with Western loans and with large Western-backed industrial projects. In order to keep down the unemployment level, Yugoslavs were encouraged to work abroad. By 1970 there were 400,000 working in West Germany alone. The Yugoslav economy greatly benefited from the hard currency earnings that the workers sent home from abroad. Additional income was obtained from the massive tourist industry along the Adriatic coast. In 1970, Yugoslavia was the destination of 5 million vacationers.

During the 1970s, the weak foundations of the Yugoslav economy were exposed. The trade imbalance grew, and Tito was obliged to go, cap in hand, to Western bankers to obtain more loans. By 1979, Yugoslavia owed between 10 and 12 billion dollars to the West; the country had to borrow abroad simply to pay off the annual interest on the debt. Ignoring Tito's appeals for restraint, workers' councils contin-

The differences in wealth among the various peoples of Yugoslavia, which became greater in the 1970s, were part of the causes of the conflict that broke out in the 1990s.

Tourists from Western Europe enjoyed sun, sand, and cheap vacations in Yugoslavia. During the 1970s a massive tourist industry was built up around destinations such as Split (shown here) and Dubrovnik.

ually voted themselves higher wages. As a result, inflation grew to over 30 percent per year, destroying the profits of many firms. Even though there were more Yugoslavs working abroad than ever before, unemployment rose rapidly, to include almost a sixth of the workforce.

Tito had hoped that prosperity would heal the wounds of the past: Instead of thinking of themselves as Croats, Slovenes, or Serbs, the peoples of Yugoslavia would think of themselves as being first and foremost consumers. However, the 1970s saw not just economic failure, but the reopening of older national divisions and rivalries.

Although Tito had created new industries in the poorer regions of Yugoslavia, the gap between the poorer and wealthier parts of the country actually widened in the 1970s. On average, a Slovene now earned twice the wage of a Serb and more than three times as much as a Macedonian or Montenegrin. As the economy declined, the wealthier Croats and Slovenes became increasingly resentful of the way they were expected to subsidize the poorer parts of Yugoslavia. By contrast, many Serbs, Montenegrins, and Macedonians believed that they deserved more assistance from the Slovenes and Croats than they had so far received.

Being the capital of Croatia, Zagreb was one of the most affluent parts of the country, and its inhabitants were cushioned from the harsher realities of life in rural parts of the country. However, agitation in 1971 for a more independent Croatia was firmly suppressed by President Tito.

The Croats were the noisiest in their complaints. In 1971, there were demonstrations in the Croatian capital, Zagreb, that were joined by leading Croatian members of the Communist party. The demands of the protesters escalated from economic justice (banners read STOP THE PLUNDER OF CROATIA) to calls for an independent Croatia. Tito reacted firmly. He arrested 400 protesters, imprisoned the leaders of the demonstrations, and got rid of the local Communist party chiefs.

Nevertheless, nationalist demands continued to be voiced everywhere in Yugoslavia. As a consequence of the renewed nationalist agitation, Tito agreed, in 1974, to a drastic reorganization of the Yugoslav state. In a new constitution adopted that year, the power of the central government in Belgrade was drastically cut back. Responsibility for decision making was

> The Yugoslav constitution of 1974 was one of the longest and most complicated in the world. Its text ran to over 300 printed pages.

given to the six republican governments (in Serbia, Croatia, Slovenia, Bosnia-Herzegovina, Macedonia, and Montenegro). In the republic of Serbia, increased powers were given to two autonomous provinces: the Vojvodina, where a large Hungarian minority lived; and Kosovo, which had a majority Albanian population.

Tito hoped that the new constitution would meet national demands for self-government halfway. Once given power, however, the new provincial governments only wanted more. The Albanians of Kosovo, who had long been the poorest part of all Yugoslavia, demanded furthermore that their autonomous province be made into a full republic. Serbs, for their part, resented the way their republic had been broken up into three parts by Tito. The constitution of 1974 thus only served to widen divisions in the country.

Despite the failure of his policies, throughout his lifetime Tito enjoyed enormous prestige in Yugoslavia. Schoolchildren in Yugoslavia seldom learned any modern history other than the story of how Tito had organized the partisans and defeated the Germans. With his private palaces, yachts, limousines, and medal-bedecked uniforms, Tito had all the trappings of a monarch. While he lived, his reputation and occasional ruthlessness proved sufficient to keep Yugoslavia together. In 1980, however, after a long illness, Tito died.

Tito held the office of secretary-general of the Yugoslav Communist party from 1937 until his death in 1980. In 1953 Tito created for himself the office of president of Yugoslavia and was later made president for life. Although claiming to be a communist, Tito lived in a lavish style and took particular pleasure in his luxury cars, trains, yachts, and island villas. Many Yugoslavs respected him all the more for his "royal" appearance.

THE RISE OF SLOBODAN MILOŠEVIĆ

After his death in 1980, Tito's place was taken by a "revolving presidency." Instead of there being a single president for the whole of Yugoslavia, representatives of each of Yugoslavia's six republics and two provinces took it in turn to be president of Yugoslavia for a year at a time. The system of the revolving presidency amounted to admission of the fact that a united Yugoslavia had not been established and that the various republics, provinces, and peoples of Yugoslavia still nursed deep suspicions of one another.

Yugoslavia did not share in the economic upturn that benefited most of the rest of Europe in the 1980s. Instead, the country's foreign debt continued to grow, soon reaching 20 billion dollars. As Western bankers grew tired of supporting the Yugoslav economy, the government was forced to borrow money even from China. The situation worsened as governments and banks in the individual republics of Yugoslavia took out loans of their own. The country was completely awash in "make-believe" money, which had been borrowed rather than earned. By the end of the decade, the annual inflation rate in Yugoslavia had risen to between 2,000 and 3,000 percent per year.

A major area of government spending was the autonomous province of Kosovo in Serbia. The population of Kosovo consisted mainly of Muslim Albanians, and the region was the poorest in the whole of Yugoslavia. Heavy unemployment affected young people in particular. Serbs, Montenegrins, and Macedonians became fearful that the Albanians of Kosovo would rebel and might even seek to join up with the neighboring communist state of Albania. In 1981 there were riots in Kosovo's

Standing alone. Slobodan Milošević, president of Serbia (far right), at a meeting with the presidents of Croatia, Slovenia, Bosnia-Herzegovina, and Macedonia in April 1991. Within a few months, troops loyal to Milošević were at war in Croatia and Slovenia.

The impoverished province of Kosovo, with its largely Muslim population, was presented by Slobodan Milošcvić as a major threat to the Serbian people and state. Milošević's appeal to Serbian nationalism and his subsequent persecution of Kosovo's Muslims spread alarm throughout the non-Serbian republics of Yugoslavia.

capital, Pristina, involving Albanian students, schoolchildren, and workers. As a consequence, huge amounts of money were pumped into Kosovo in order to create jobs for the Albanians and to make them feel less discontented.

Considerable resentment grew in Serbia about the situation in Kosovo. The rapid growth of the Albanian population was seen as a threat by the Serbs who lived in the province and who, in the main, had the better-paid jobs. From almost a quarter of the population in 1960, the Serbs had been reduced to just over 10 percent two decades later. Continued unrest in Kosovo, involving alleged attacks by Muslim Albanians on Serbian families, churches, and businesses, spread considerable alarm throughout Serbia.

Kosovo had, furthermore, always been a place dear to the hearts of Serbs. In 1389, the army of the medieval Serbian kingdom was destroyed by a Muslim Turkish army at a battle fought on the Field of Blackbirds in Kosovo. Memory of this catastrophe awakened fears among the Serbs that they would be overcome once again by sheer force of Muslim numbers.

These fears were exploited by the leader of the Serbian Communists and president of the republic, Slobodan Milošević. Although a life-long Communist and former close supporter of Tito, Milošević now presented himself as the champion of the Serbian people. Beginning in 1987, Milošević argued that the Yugoslavia created by Tito after World War II was a fraud that discriminated against the Serbian people. He claimed that the Albanians of Kosovo had

The Albanians of Kosovo
"Ninety per cent of Kosovo's population of 1.7 million are Albanians (also known as Shqiptars) and speak that language, and most of them are Muslim. According to Serbian propaganda, there were as many Serbs as Albanians in Kosovo a generation ago, but the majority of Serbs were driven out by Albanian terrorism. None of this is true: Kosovo has been solidly Albanian for centuries, and those of its Serbian minority who left did so to find greener pastures in the north."

(*Eastern Europe 1939–1989*, Patrick Brogan, 1990)

already been granted far too many privileges at the expense of the Serbian population. Milošević organized massive demonstrations in Kosovo protesting alleged Albanian "atrocities" against the local Serbian population. In 1989, a rally to commemorate the 600th anniversary of the Field of Blackbirds was attended by more than a million Serbs waving banners in support of Milosević's tough stand.

Having whipped up considerable popular backing from the Serbian population of Yugoslavia, Milošević put through a series of sweeping constitutional changes. First, he abolished the special rights of the autonomous provinces of Kosovo and Vojvodina. Second, he organized demonstrations in neighboring Montenegro, which resulted in the collapse of the republic's government. All the top offices in Kosovo, Vojvodina, and Montenegro were then filled with supporters of the Serbian president.

Milošević's rise to power was watched with alarm in Slovenia and Croatia. It seemed that Milošević was trying to turn Yugoslavia into a state dominated by Serbs and by his own followers. Milošević's use of Serbian nationalism as a political rallying point resulted in a backlash against the Serbs in Slovenia and Croatia. Croatian and Slovenian leaders

1989: Timetable of revolutions in Eastern Europe	
August	Poland: non-Communist prime minister appointed
October	Hungary: Communist party collapses
November	East Germany: Berlin Wall breached
November	Bulgaria: Communist leader arrested
November	Czechoslovakia: Communist government overthrown in "Velvet Revolution"
December	Romania: Communist leader overthrown and executed

By the end of the year, only two communist governments remained in power in Eastern Europe: in Albania and Yugoslavia.

demanded that their own republics be granted additional powers of self-government to protect them against what they saw as the swelling tide of Serbian intolerance.

In 1989, Communist power in Eastern Europe collapsed. Throughout Eastern Europe free elections were held that resulted in the formation of democratic, non-Communist governments. Yugoslavia could not remain isolated from the changes affecting the rest of Eastern

Commemorating the 600th anniversary of the defeat of the Serbian army in Kosovo in 1389, these modern-day Serbs hold up a banner of their leader, Slobodan Milošević.

A Muslim, demonstrating in March 1989 against the abolition of the special status of Kosovo province, is arrested by Serbian police. Over the next few years, only a huge police presence prevented further widespread disorder in Kosovo.

Europe. Demands grew for free elections and for the establishment of a democratic system that would rescue the country from its economic mess.

The Communist party of Yugoslavia proved, however, incapable of agreeing on whether or how a more democratic system should be introduced. At its last congress, held at the beginning of 1990, the Yugoslav Communist party fell apart, and no decisions on the future of the country were reached.

In this way, economic chaos was joined by political chaos. Neither the Communist party nor the government in Belgrade was any longer capable of offering leadership. Frightened that Milošević would exploit the political vacuum to increase his powers still further, the Slovene and Croatian Communists decided to go their own way entirely and to hold free elections in their republics. The Croatian and Slovene

Communists believed that they could hold out against Milošević more effectively if they could show that they had the support of the voters in the two republics. They also reckoned that their defiance would ensure them sufficient backing to win the elections. As it turned out, the Croatian and Slovene Communists were completely mistaken.

> **Speech by Slobodan Milošević to the Serbian parliament, March 1991**
> "Serbia and the Serb people are faced with one of the greatest evils of their history: the challenge of disunity and internal conflict. . . . All who love Serbia dare not ignore this fact, especially at a time when we are confronted by the vampiroid, fascistic forces of the *Ustaša*, Albanian secessionists and all other forces in the anti-Serbian coalition which threatens the people's rights and freedoms."
>
> (*The Fall of Yugoslavia*, Misha Glenny, 1992)

DISINTEGRATION AND WAR

In the spring of 1990, free elections were held in Slovenia and Croatia. In both republics, the Communists were beaten by newly formed right-wing parties. In Croatia, the winning party was the Croatian Democratic Union, led by General Franjo Tudjman, a former partisan and Communist. Free elections were held later that year in Bosnia-Herzegovina and in Macedonia, also resulting in wins for nationalist parties.

The defeat of the Communists alarmed Milošević, who, besides being president of Serbia, was also head of the Serbian Communist party. Accordingly, he renamed the party the Socialist party and played down his previous role as a

Franjo Tudjman
Born in Croatia in 1922, Tudjman fought with Tito in World War II, becoming the youngest partisan general. After the war he remained in the Communist party and took up work as a historian. Under his direction, the University of Zagreb was purged of non-Communists in the late 1940s and 1950s. Because of the support he showed in 1971 for Croatian independence, Tudjman was placed under house arrest and later jailed. Although now claiming to have spent the 1970s and 1980s as a political prisoner, for most of this time Tudjman was in fact living in a luxury villa in the suburbs of Zagreb.

Ex-Communist turned Croatian patriot, Franjo Tudjman (center) visits the front in August 1991.

Although all Yugoslav men were obliged to undergo training in the army, few were prepared either militarily or psychologically for the fierce conflict that erupted in June 1991. Most believed that Milošević and the politicians were bluffing and would never use force to achieve their goals.

Communist leader. More and more he posed as the defender of the Serbian people against Albanians, Croats, Slovenes, and Muslims. He presented the other peoples of Yugoslavia as enemies of the Serbs and claimed that they were plotting a war of genocide against the Serbs.

Milošević's ruthless tactics of deception were sufficient to win him complete control of Serbia in elections held in November 1990. His followers also won a decisive victory in Montenegro.

Communist power therefore collapsed entirely in the elections held in the republics of Yugoslavia during 1990. In every republic, first place went to those politicians who emphasized their importance as leaders, not of the Yugoslav people as a whole, but instead of just one of Yugoslavia's peoples. The elections of 1990 showed that nationalism was once again by far the most powerful force in the country's politics.

Once released, nationalism became hard to control. Although serious attempts were made by non-Serb politicians to keep Yugoslavia together, their fear of Serbia and their distrust of Milošević worked against a solution being found. Furthermore, the newly elected politicians proved as incapable as their predecessors of solving the economic problems. As a result, they increasingly played on nationalist fears as a way of bolstering up public support. After a last-ditch attempt to reach a compromise failed in the summer of 1991, Slovenia and Croatia declared their full independence. Macedonia followed at the end of the year, and Bosnia-Herzegovina did the same in early 1992. In all four republics, referendums were organized to make sure that the declarations of independence had the support of the majority of the population.

Serbia and Montenegro, however, did not follow the pattern of the other republics and did not set themselves up as fully independent states. Instead they remained part of Yugoslavia. Milošević and his supporters argued that the other republics had no right to leave Yugoslavia and that their declarations of independence were therefore illegal. At the Serbs' instructions, the Yugoslav army was sent into Slovenia, in June 1991, to try to stop the republic from setting itself up as a completely independent state. However, having encountered more resistance than anticipated, the army was quickly withdrawn.

Milošević was, as it turned out, ready to let Slovenia go. Croatia, however, was a different matter. More than 10 percent of Croatia's population consisted of Serbs, who were mainly concentrated in eastern Slavonia and in Krajina. In 1991, the Serbs living in Krajina held their own referendum and voted to leave Croatia.

Milošević was trapped. He had built his reputation as the champion of the Serbs. How could he now let the Serbs of Krajina remain in the "foreign" and "illegal" republic of Croatia when they so obviously wanted to join Serbia? But the Croatian president, General Tudjman, was caught, too. As the newly elected leader of Croatia, how could he agree, as his first major political act, to give away a part of Croatia? With no room for a compromise, and with both Tudjman and Milošević deeply suspicious of each other, war became inevitable.

In August 1991, the "Yugoslav" army, which by now consisted mainly of Serbian and Montenegrin troops, went on the offensive in Croatia. The Croatians did not have an army of their own and so at first had to put lightly armed policemen into battle. Superior in both weapons and manpower, the Yugoslav army pushed the Croatian forces out of the disputed areas, inflicting huge casualties and devastation. In order to force the Croatians to submit, the Yugoslav army shelled the ancient port of Dubrovnik, and its air force bombed the center of Zagreb, even though neither city had any military significance.

In January 1992 the Croatian government agreed to a cease-fire that left 30 percent of Croatia occupied by the Serbian "Yugoslav" army. In the area of occupation, the Serbs immediately embarked on a policy of "ethnic

---

War songs

A Croatian war song
A battle is being fought,
The Croatian banner is flying
For freedom and our home,
For the Croat home.

A Serbian war song
A battle is being fought,
The heroic banner is flying
For the freedom of Serbia,
For the Serbian home.

(Both songs are sung to the same tune.)

Six hundred tanks and 30,000 troops devastated the Croatian city of Vukovar in a siege lasting from September to November 1991. The loss of Vukovar is recalled today in many of the names given to Croatian streets.

Victims of ethnic cleansing often had to be "housed" in makeshift refugee camps that lacked water, electricity, and sanitary facilities. Many refugees owed their lives to the exceptional mildness of the winter of 1992–1993.

cleansing": driving out the Croatian population and giving over their homes to Serbs. Resort hotels along the Adriatic coast became refuges for many thousands of Croatian families.

Tudjman was much criticized in Croatia, first for allowing his country to go to war so unprepared and second for agreeing to a cease-fire that left more than a quarter of the country in enemy hands. In order to silence his critics, Tudjman began a policy entirely in keeping with his background as a Communist leader. He closed down the newspapers that opposed him, allowing only progovernment papers to be published; took over the radio and television stations; and ordered the arrest of political opponents on trumped-up charges. Outside Croatia, however, few noticed Tudjman's repression. Instead, the attention of the world was increasingly focused on the unfolding tragedy in Bosnia-Herzegovina.

Milošević reelected
In December 1992, Milošević was reelected president of Serbia, triumphing over his rival, the moderate Milan Panić. The Socialist party, of which Milošević is the leader, and the even more extreme Radical party, won 175 seats in the 250-seat Serbian parliament.

THE BOSNIAN TRAGEDY

The population of the republic of Bosnia-Herzegovina was the most mixed in all Yugoslavia. No single nationality made up a majority among the republic's 4 million inhabitants. Although Muslims were the largest group, accounting for 40 percent of the republic's total population, there were also substantial Serbian and Croatian populations. Unlike in Croatia, the various population groups were scattered throughout the republic and there was no single part of Bosnia-Herzegovina that was exclusively Muslim, Serbian, or Croatian. Many of the villages and towns of Bosnia-Herzegovina were mixed communities and had for centuries been the homes of more than one nationality.

Political leader of the Bosnian Serbs, Radovan Karadzić claims descent from one of Serbia's most famous families. Previously a psychiatrist, specializing in neurosis and depression, Dr. Karadzić did part of his medical training in London.

Following elections held at the end of 1990, the Muslim Party of Democratic Action had emerged as the largest party in the republic's parliament. The party's leader, Alija Izetbegović, had subsequently been appointed president. A year later, in November 1991, the Muslims and Croats in the parliament voted in favor of Bosnia-Herzegovina becoming a completely independent state, with its capital at Sarajevo. The decision of the parliament was subsequently approved in a referendum held in March 1992.

Although the referendum result showed that a majority of voters supported Bosnia-Herzegovina becoming independent, most Serbs boycotted the poll. Many Serbs wanted Bosnia-Herzegovina to remain a part of Yugoslavia, along with the republics of Serbia and Montenegro. A large number also nursed a deep distrust of Izetbegović. In the 1980s, Izetbegović had proclaimed himself a Muslim fundamentalist and had called for the creation of an Islamic republic in Bosnia-Herzegovina.

Muslims made up the largest population group in Bosnia-Herzegovina. From the tall towers or minarets situated in many Bosnian villages, the Muslims were called to prayer by the muezzins.

Although by 1990 Izetbegović had reversed his previous statements, saying that he now believed in a state where all religions had equal rights, many Serbs were unconvinced by his change of mind.

Izetbegović tried hard to win the confidence of the Serbian population of Bosnia-Herzegovina, even to the extent of cooperating with the Serbian-led "Yugoslav" army, following its withdrawal from Croatia at the end of 1991. His cabinet included not just Muslims but also representatives of the Serbian and Croatian communities. Izetbegović also deliberately held back from creating a Bosnian army for fear of inflaming the tense situation in the republic.

Izetbegović's moderation was not, however, rewarded. Instead, the second largest of Bosnia-Herzegovina's political parties, the Serbian Democratic party, announced plans of its own to establish an independent Serbian state in Bosnia-Herzegovina. Under the leadership of Radovan Karadzić, the Serbian Democratic party proposed that no less than two-thirds of Bosnia-Herzegovina be included in the new state. Defying the government in Sarajevo, Serbian gunmen started to take control of the areas that the Serbian Democratic party had claimed.

By April 1992, Bosnia-Herzegovina was in the grip of a full-scale war. A hastily gathered and largely Muslim army sought to maintain order in the face of attacks by Serbian fighters. The Muslims were, on the whole, supported by the local Croats, who also had no wish to see most of the republic taken over by Serbs. There were also a number of Serbs who preferred to support the properly elected government.

The war that followed was, however, far from being a civil war fought out only between the various population groups in Bosnia-Herzegovina. The Serbian forces in Bosnia-Herzegovina were given substantial assistance by the Serbian "Yugoslav" army, led initially by Milošević's chief of staff, General Blagoje Adzić. He not only supplied troops to assist the republic's Serbs, but also provided artillery and fighter planes. "Volunteer brigades" from Serbia also participated in large numbers in the conflict.

Such was the weight of military involvement

> **A description of General Adzić**
> "Medically he can be diagnosed as a paranoid psychotic. His astonishingly devious and inventive cunning, which is in marked contrast to his obvious intellectual limitations, is a typical hallmark of people in this state of mind. He shows a complete lack of moral scruples, breathtaking ruthlessness, and an absence of emotional reaction. His only facial expressions are barely controlled anger, grand gravity, or thin joviality. Again, as to be expected with a psychotic paranoid, he is driven by the grandiose, intricate and illogical masterplan to defeat 'the enemy.'"
>
> (*Eastern Europe Newsletter*, May 11, 1992)

by Serbia that Karadzić's influence declined. Although Karadzić was still portrayed as the leader of the Serbs of Bosnia-Herzegovina, real power lay in the hands of Milošević and of his

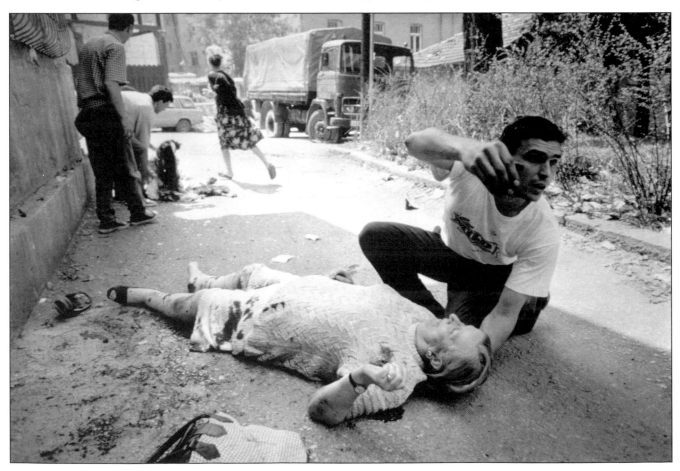

Sarajevo's civilian population was besieged by Serbian forces and constantly targeted by artillery units and snipers situated in the hills surrounding the city.

Ethnic cleansing in action: Muslims forced from their homes in the Bosnian city of Srbrenica are taken to refugee camps in United Nations trucks. They are watched by Serbian soldiers. Later on, some of these trucks were attacked by unidentified gunmen.

henchman in the republic, General Ratko Mladić. Even Milošević was frequently obliged to take into account the ambitions and wishes of the gangsters, warlords, and madmen whom the war had set loose.

The Bosnian Serbs had two goals in mind. First, they wanted to establish a large Serbian republic in Bosnia-Herzegovina that would then, so they hoped, unite with Serbia itself. Second, they wanted to establish a corridor through the north of the republic linking Serbia to those parts of Croatia that the Serbs had already occupied. In order to fulfill these two objectives, the Serbs needed to capture three-quarters of the territory of Bosnia-Herzegovina.

With the massive support provided by the Serbian republic, the Serbian fighters in Bosnia-Herzegovina rapidly pushed the Muslim forces out of the areas that they claimed. By the middle of 1992, Serbian forces were pounding Sarajevo. As the Serbian army seemed unstoppable, the Croatian government felt obliged to intervene. The Croatian army, recently equipped with French, South African, and Argentinian weapons, was ordered across the border to defend western Bosnia-Herzegovina, where a large share of the republic's Croatian population lived. Although at first cooperating with the Muslims, by the beginning of 1993 the Croatian forces were at war with the Bosnian Muslims for control of territory.

The strategy of the Serbian commanders in Bosnia-Herzegovina was straightforward. The Serbian state that they sought to create included territory where the population was still predominantly non-Serbian. If the new state was to be the truly Serbian one that they envisioned, something would have to be done about the Muslim and Croatian populations. The solution eventually adopted was the same as the one that had been followed in the regions of Serbian-occupied Croatia: "ethnic cleansing" or, in other words, the terrorizing, slaughter, and forcible eviction of all those who were not Serbs.

Sarajevo

The Serbian siege of Sarajevo began in April 1992. The city's 400,000 inhabitants included 90,000 Serbs who remained loyal to their republic's elected government.

CHAPTER 9

RAPE AND REFUGEES

The fighting in Croatia and in Bosnia-Herzegovina was accompanied by much brutality. All sides massacred civilians and executed prisoners of war. Stories of atrocities led immediately to reprisals and then to further revenge killings. The news media throughout the republics of former Yugoslavia carried daily—and often highly colored—reports of the enemy's misdeeds. The distrust felt by each population group for the other made it easy to believe that the enemy was capable of performing any outrage.

The fighting in former Yugoslavia was particularly savage because of the way all sides relied upon ill-disciplined volunteers. The Croatian army was assisted by black-shirted militiamen, sporting swastikas and crucifixes, who openly proclaimed themselves to be fascist *Ustaša*. Eventually, in the autumn of 1992, the Croatian army was obliged to rein in the militias, shooting several of their leaders. For their part, the Serbs fighting in Bosnia-Herzegovina were aided by "weekend Rambos." These were workers from Serbia who spent their free time terrorizing the Bosnian countryside while dressed for effect in headbands and cartridge belts. There were also full-time Serbian volunteers, organized in brigades, variously called the Chetniks, Tigers, and White Eagles. Serbian volunteers, high on alcohol, stimulants, and stories of atrocities, frequently committed the vilest excesses on the civilian population of Bosnia-Herzegovina.

Although both Muslims and Croats carried out many atrocities, the Serbian forces undoubtedly committed the worst. This was

The Serbian army enjoyed a substantial advantage in the fighting since it took over most of the arms and equipment of the Yugoslav Federal Army.

Muslim and Croatian men in Bosnia were routinely imprisoned in camps run by the Serbian army, police, and volunteers. Foreign journalists and aid workers were only admitted to the most orderly and well run camps, like this one.

mainly due to the policy of "ethnic cleansing" adopted by the Serbian commanders in the field and by their political masters in Belgrade.

In order to create areas that were entirely Serb, and thus likely to vote to join Serbia once the fighting was over, the Serbian forces embarked upon the wholesale removal of the non-Serbian population. This policy was first begun in 1991 in the Serbian-occupied parts of Croatia and was continued over the next two years in Bosnia-Herzegovina.

In the territory that they captured, the Serbs immediately began terrorizing the local non-Serb population. Croats and Muslims were frequently given the choice of fleeing or watching their homes being burned. Elsewhere, they were fired from their jobs, obliged to wear identifying arm bands, or compelled to pay "protection money." In order to encourage the departure of the non-Serbian population, random executions were organized, with the victims often being tortured before death. These atrocities were committed not only by the volunteer brigades from afar, but also by the victims' former friends and neighbors.

Since the nature of the fighting meant that in many places the non-Serbian population had nowhere to flee, they were often rounded up and placed in any one of many detention camps. Some of these camps, which were often administered by volunteers, assumed the appearance of death camps. This was rarely

Ethnic cleansing

"We all come from Kozarac, a small Muslim town in northern Bosnia. The Serbs occupied our town, killing, robbing and raping. Then they blew up our houses, leaving us only with what we could carry ourselves."

(Bosnian refugee to United Nations official, 1992)

Murder of prisoners in Serbian detention camps

"As far as is known, the killing is mostly by gunshot, though the slitting of throats is the preferred Chetnik ritual. Vicious beatings, often apparently at random, with anything from boots to iron bars, and in many cases to death, is the most frequently reported torture. Mutilation with a knife is a recurrent feature. The Chetniks have a strange penchant for slashing off ears and noses. . . . There is reliable testimony that Imams [Muslim priests] are singled out for torture and execution—several hundred are reported to have been killed, some by torture medievals would have been proud of."

(*Eastern Europe Newsletter*, August 10, 1992)

their purpose, but in the camps the half-starved inmates were casually subjected to much violence. Although reliable estimates of the number of persons killed in the camps are unavailable, the death toll must be measured in the thousands.

Reports that the Serbs in Bosnia-Herzegovina were practicing what amounted to genocide in the detention camps resulted in the most spectacular propaganda "failures" of the conflict. In order to convince the outside world that no such policy was being pursued, the Serbs allowed Western journalists to visit the detention camp at Omarska in August 1992. Films of the camp's emaciated and beaten inmates shocked television viewers throughout the world and brought home for the first time the true

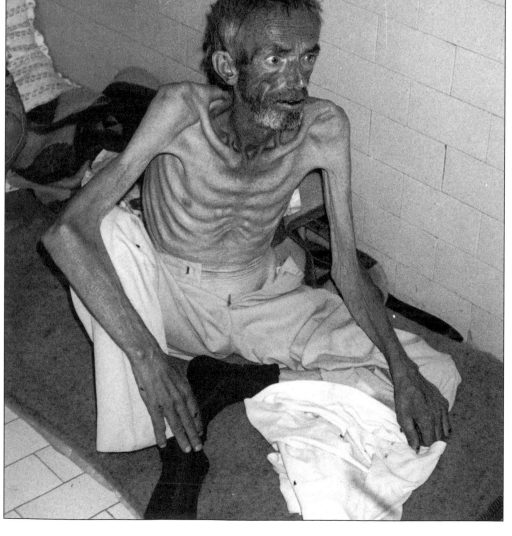

Many civilian prisoners in Serbian-run detention camps were denied proper food and medicine. Some, like this man, were systematically starved; others were beaten and even killed.

Serbian soldiers and volunteers frequently raped Muslim women and girls, intending to make them unfit to be wives or mothers. These three victims of rape console one another as they tell their horrific stories to Western journalists.

brutality of the Serbian offensive in Bosnia-Herzegovina.

While the men of Bosnia-Herzegovina were rounded up into camps, the women suffered a perhaps even more cruel fate. Throughout the preceding years, the Serbian population had been fed stories about the threat posed to them by the high Muslim birth rate. Upon capturing a Muslim area, Serbian soldiers and volunteers would systematically rape women and young girls in order to make them unfit, in the eyes of Muslim men, to be either wives or mothers. It is estimated that possibly as many as 40,000 Muslim girls and women, with ages ranging from nine to over sixty, have been raped. The more attractive women were sometimes put in brothels. It is alleged that at the "Cafe Sonja" brothel in the hills above Sarajevo, Muslim women were made available to Serbian soldiers in week-long shifts, after which they were shot.

Many Serbs believe that similar places in which Serbian women are raped are run by Muslims.

The violence in Bosnia-Herzegovina released a flood of refugees. It is estimated that by the end of 1992, more than 1.5 million people, over a third of the republic's total population, had either left or lost their homes.

In terror for their own lives, Croats and Serbs who found themselves on the wrong side of the lines fled to Croatia and Serbia in large numbers. The Muslims, however, had nowhere safe to go. They crowded instead into the cramped cities that the Serbian forces had not yet taken. In Sarajevo, Tuzla, Goražde, and Srbrenica, the terrified refugees found, however, little safety. Blockaded by Serbian forces, the refugee-swollen cities had insufficient food and shelter. Furthermore, the Serbs continued to pound the refugees with their artillery. It continued to be the aim of the Serbian forces to capture these cities and to drive out their populations as the first step in creating a pure, "ethnically cleansed" Serbian state in Bosnia-Herzegovina.

Some Muslims tried to escape the fighting and starvation by fleeing into the western part of Bosnia-Herzegovina, which had been occupied by the Croatian army. The Croats, however, resisted the influx of refugees. As a consequence, fierce fighting erupted in 1993 between Croats and Muslims in the city of Mostar.

Refugees

By the end of 1992 there were more than 2 million homeless people in former Yugoslavia and an additional half million refugees living abroad.

THE SEARCH FOR A SOLUTION

The war in former Yugoslavia was the first major war in Europe since 1945. The rapidity with which fighting broke out clearly surprised Western politicians and diplomats. Convinced that Yugoslavia was really a civilized and sophisticated European country, they did not believe that the various sides would ever do more than argue and bluster. They therefore ignored the increasingly pessimistic and urgent reports sent in by their secret intelligence services, most notably the Central Intelligence Agency (CIA), which warned of the danger of armed conflict.

Throughout 1990 and 1991, Western politicians tried to keep Yugoslavia together. They argued that if Yugoslavia was allowed to break up, this might give a signal to the republics of the increasingly feeble Soviet Union to declare their own independence. By supporting the continued existence of Yugoslavia, Western politicians in fact only encouraged President Milošević to adopt a hard line in response to the Slovenian and Croatian declarations of independence. Nor, as it turned out, did their policy prevent the disintegration of the Soviet Union.

Ever since World War II, the United States had assisted as a guardian and peacekeeper in Europe. With the end of the cold war and the defeat of communism, the Americans saw less reason why they should be so heavily involved in European affairs. The American government therefore entrusted the solution of the "Yugoslav problem" to the European Community (EC). At this time the EC was presenting itself as the most important force in European politics. Although Yugoslavia was not a member of the EC, it was seen as lying very much in the community's own "backyard."

In August 1991, representatives of the EC

Amid much celebration, Croatia and Slovenia declared independence in the summer of 1991. It was six months, however, before the European Community recognized Croatia and Slovenia as independent states.

The first UN troops arrived in the former Yugoslavia in early 1992. These French soldiers joined a force including troops from a variety of countries. All the UN forces, however, found themselves powerless to control the bitter fighting in Serbian-occupied Croatia.

declared that they could no longer "stand idly by" as the fighting in the former Yugoslavia raged. Accordingly, they held a series of peace talks with leaders of the various peoples and republics of the former Yugoslavia. The talks were joined by representatives of the United Nations (UN), the international body charged with the duty of preventing armed conflict.

As a result of their discussions, held while the fighting in Croatia was still going on, the member states of the EC decided at the end of 1991 to recognize Slovenia and Croatia as independent states. Bosnia-Herzegovina was told to stage a vote on independence, after which it, too, might be recognized. At the same time, the UN organized a cease-fire between Croatia and Serbia. It was agreed that 14,000 UN troops should

be sent into the Serbian-occupied parts of Croatia. The Serbian forces would then withdraw from these parts, and Croatian refugees would be allowed to return to their homes.

Macedonia
Although ready to recognize Slovenia, Croatia, and Bosnia-Herzegovina, the EC failed to recognize Macedonia as an independent state. This was because representatives of the Greek government vetoed recognition on the curious grounds that Macedonia was also the name of a part of Greece. By April 1993, however, a workable compromise had been reached: Macedonia would be known and recognized as the Former Yugoslav Republic of Macedonia.

As it turned out, the UN Protection Force (UNPROFOR) sent into the Serbian-occupied parts of Croatia failed entirely to do its job. Even in the areas designated UN Protection Areas (UNPAs), Serbian forces continued to practice ethnic cleansing—in full view of the UN troops. No attempt was made by the UN to restore the occupied areas to Croatian control as had previously been agreed. When, in January 1993, the Croatian army seized the site of a strategically vital bridge from the Serbian army, the local detachment of UN troops simply fled. A number of UNPROFOR units, including Nigerian, Polish, and Russian troops, also engaged in black-marketing and smuggling, as well as charging refugees large sums of money for safe passage.

In November 1991, the UN and the EC organized economic sanctions against Serbia in the hope of forcing its government to give up its support of the war. Although sanctions did have some effect, they were insufficiently enforced. Serbia continued to obtain supplies through Ukraine, Greece, and Romania. Even though patrolled by UN troops, refineries in the UNPAs also sent oil quite openly to Serbia.

The EC and the UN were additionally involved in trying to negotiate a settlement for Bosnia-Herzegovina that would put an end to the fighting. In autumn 1992, the EC and UN representatives, the former British foreign secretary Lord Owen and the former American secretary of state Cyrus Vance, announced a plan to divide Bosnia-Herzegovina up into ten largely self-governing provinces. The boundaries of the provinces were designed so that each

For more than twelve months, EC and UN peace negotiators tried to work out a political solution in Bosnia-Herzegovina that would bring an end to the fighting. The negotiations were led for much of 1992–1993 by the former British foreign secretary, Lord Owen (right), and the former U.S. secretary of state, Cyrus Vance (left).

Dividing up Bosnia-Herzegovina into ten largely self-governing provinces was one of the proposals put forward by the EC-UN negotiators. The plan was resisted by all the parties in the conflict and had to be abandoned in the summer of 1993. A new plan to divide Bosnia-Herzegovina into three ministates—one each for the Bosnian Muslims, Serbs, and Croats—proved equally short-lived.

would allow one population group to form a majority. (The province of Sarajevo would, however, remain mixed, without any one nationality forming a majority.)

The Owen-Vance plan only served to make the conflict worse. Before the boundaries of the provinces became finalized, each side tried to grab as much land as possible. The Serbian army redoubled its bombardment of the Muslim cities in central and eastern Bosnia to demonstrate that these centers would eventually be parts of Serbian provinces. Croatian forces, for their part, began brutally expelling Muslims from the parts of the republic that they controlled. At the time,

however, the Owen-Vance plan was thought the only practical solution to which all sides might agree.

The hardships experienced by the Muslim population of Bosnia-Herzegovina resulted in the establishment of a second UN force. Made up this time of well-disciplined British, Canadian, Spanish, and French troops, the task of this 6,000-strong UN force in Bosnia-Herzegovina was to get relief supplies to the trapped Muslim cities. A large-scale airlift ferried food to the besieged capital, Sarajevo. Nevertheless, with orders to engage only in humanitarian work, the UN troops in Bosnia-Herzegovina were left at the mercy of local Serbian and Croatian commanders. Serbs and Croats frequently refused to allow convoys to reach the starving Muslim population; relief trucks were often the targets of sniper and mortar fire.

The inability of the EC and of the UN either to negotiate a political settlement in the former Yugoslavia or to prevent famine, rape, and "ethnic cleansing" in Bosnia-Herzegovina led to repeated calls for decisive Western military action against Serbia. Although the war in former Yugoslavia involved atrocities not seen in Europe since Auschwitz, it must be understood that countries only rarely go to war for humanitarian reasons. Politicians may be fond of talking of principles and of morality, but they will seldom intervene abroad militarily except for reasons of their own national interest. The rugged terrain of

UN convoys bringing relief supplies to the besieged cities of Bosnia-Herzegovina were frequently stopped by Serbian and Croatian roadblocks. On occasion, aid convoys were also fired upon.

A makeshift cemetery outside Sarajevo. By the summer of 1993 it was clear that Western Europe was unwilling to intervene in Bosnia Herzegovina and that the slaughter was therefore likely to continue.

Bosnia-Herzegovina and the ferocious nature of the fighting made it seem likely that intervention would result in many thousands of casualties.

Unwilling to put the lives of their own soldiers at risk, politicians and diplomats in Western Europe continued to advocate policies of "restraint" and "limited engagement" even as the suffering and fighting worsened in 1993. In so doing, however, they revealed that the EC was unable to perform the basic peacekeeping role in European affairs that it had tried to take over from the Americans only two years before.

The failure of Western policy and its implications
"The continued inability of the European Community and most Western powers individually to devise a credible strategy towards the Balkan war heralds an escalating diplomatic and foreign policy shambles. . . . The mixture of Western inertia, misreading of Balkan politics and incompetence, has greatly reduced Western standing as far as Moscow. . . . Post-communist governments, whether in Budapest, Sofia or Warsaw, cannot afford to voice criticisms into the face of the EC or other Western government representatives. In private, however, the West's utter failure to implement a workable foreign policy towards the Balkans has cast much doubt on the political future of the European Community."
(Eastern European Newsletter, August 10, 1992)

GLOSSARY

Auschwitz   The most notorious of the death camps run by the Nazis during World War II.

Autonomous   Self-governing.

Balkans   Southeastern Europe, including the countries of former Yugoslavia, Albania, Bulgaria, Greece, and Romania.

Black-marketing   Illegal trading of goods or money that are in short supply.

Chetnik   The Serbian word for a member of a *četa* or regiment. The first Chetniks fought as guerrillas against the Turks. The term was later used in World War II to refer to those Serbs who fought to restore the Serb-dominated monarchy.

Cold War   A situation that existed from 1945 to the 1980s, between Western Europe and the United States on one side and the Soviet Union and Eastern Europe on the other, when relations between the two sides were as bad as they could be without actual war breaking out.

Collectives   Large farms and businesses run and owned by the state.

Communist   A believer in communism. Communism teaches that the state should control the economy in the interests of making a society where there is no inequality.

Constitution   A group of laws laying down how a country or state is organized and governed.

Detention camp   A prison where people are held without trial.

Dictator   An absolute ruler of a country or state. Dictators often suppress a democratic government.

Ethnic cleansing   Forcible removal from an area of all people belonging to another nationality.

Fascist   A believer in fascism, which is a system of extremely authoritarian views or government.

Genocide   The deliberate destruction of a whole people or nation.

Hard currency   Money that can be used to buy goods made in the West. (Most Western governments and businesses refused to deal in East European "soft currencies" because there was nothing they wanted to buy with that money.)

Militia   A type of military force, raised from the ordinary population and helping the regular army during an emergency.

Muslim fundamentalist   A Muslim who believes in the creation of states that are governed by the teachings of the Muslim religion.

Nation   A population group usually sharing the same language and culture.

Nationalism   The belief that the world is organized into nations, that allegiance to one's own nation should take first place above all other loyalties, and that the best form of state is the nation-state.

Nation-state   A state in which members of a single nation, or nationality, make up nearly all the state's population.

Partisan   Guerrilla fighter. In Yugoslavia during World War II, partisan meant a fighter who supported Tito.

Partition   To divide a country up among its neighboring states.

Puppet government   A government that holds little power of its own and does simply what it is told to do.

Purge   Removal of political opponents.

Regent   A person entrusted with the duties of a monarch, usually because the king or queen is too young.

Rigged election   An election that is not managed honestly, so the result does not reflect the true wishes of the real majority of voters.

Sanctions   Stopping or restricting trade with a country.

Secession   When part of a state breaks away from the rest of the state.

Show trial   A trial that is arranged purely for propaganda purposes and in which the verdict has been decided in advance.

Soviet bloc   The group of communist countries formed under the leadership of the Soviet Union after World War II. In 1955, the Soviet bloc was organized in a military alliance known as the Warsaw Pact.

Subsidize   To give subsidies or financial support to someone.

Trade imbalance   When the value of a country's imports exceeds the value of its exports.

Ustaša   Croatian fascist; now a term of abuse for all Croats.

FURTHER INFORMATION

History and contemporary affairs

For more recent events, visit your local library which will have back copies of newspapers on reels of microfilm. You will need to ask a librarian to fetch the reels and to show you how to use the microfilm reader.

The history of Yugoslavia and of the South Slav peoples is given in detail in:
Singleton, Fred *A Short History of the Yugoslav Peoples*, (Cambridge University Press, 1985). Despite its title, this book is over 300 pages long.
Jelavich, Barbara *History of the Balkans*, two volumes, (Cambridge University Press, 1983).
Singleton, Fred *Twentieth-century Yugoslavia*, (Macmillan, 1976).

Biographies of Tito include:
Auty, Phyllis *Tito: A Biography*, (Harmondsworth, 1974).
Beloff, Nora *Tito's Flawed Legacy*, (Victor Gollancz Ltd, 1985). More critical and up to date.

The recent history of Yugoslavia is covered in:
Cviic, Christopher *Remaking the Balkans*, (Royal Institute of International Affairs and Pinter Publishers, 1991).
Yugofax: Breakdown – War and Reconstruction in Yugoslavia (Institute for War and Peace Reporting, 1992).

The tragic history of the war in Yugoslavia is admirably covered in two exciting accounts written by journalists:
Glenny, Misha *The Fall of Yugoslavia: The Third Balkan War*, (Penguin, 1992).
Thompson, Mark *A Paper House: The Ending of Yugoslavia*, (Hutchinson Radius, 1992).

Besides newspapers, there are also journals which analyze the contemporary situation in the former Yugoslavia. The most reliable of these are *Radio Free Europe/Radio Liberty Research Report, Balkan War Report* (also variously published as *Yugofax* and *Ex-Yugofax*), Economist Intelligence Unit *Country Report: Yugoslav Republics*, and *Eastern Europe Newsletter*. These will only be available at the largest public libraries; your local library should, however, be able to order them for you or obtain photocopies.

Literature

The works of the Nobel-Prize winner, Ivo Andrić (1892–1975) are widely translated into English. A Bosnian Serb, Andrić mainly wrote historical novels, of which *The Bridge on the Drina* is his most famous. Some short stories of the less well-known Croatian novelist, Miroslav Krleža (1893–1981), have also been translated, most notably *The Cricket Beneath the Waterfall and Other Stories*, (1972). Slavenka Drakulić's *Balkan Express: Fragments from the Other Side of War*, (Hutchinson, 1993), powerfully describes her experiences in contemporary war-torn Croatia. The most useful guide to the literature of former Yugoslavia is *The Everyman Companion to East European Literature*, edited by Robert Pynsent and Sonia Kanikova, (J.M. Dent, 1993), which provides information on almost two hundred Serb, Croat, Slovene and Macedonian authors. Inter-war Yugoslavia is vividly captured in Rebecca West's massive *Black Lamb and Grey Falcon* (1942 and many subsequent editions).

Films

A video cassette, *Timewatch: Tito* (produced by Peter Batty, 1992) including archive footage and interviews, is available from the BBC.

INDEX

DATE